CHICKWEED WINTERGREEN

PORTRAIT OF HARRY MARTINSON BY LENNART NILSSON (1956)

HARRY MARTINSON
CHICKWEED WINTERGREEN
SELECTED POEMS

TRANSLATED BY
ROBIN FULTON

INTRODUCTION BY
STAFFAN SÖDERBLOM

ERIC
BLOO
DAXE

BLOODAXE BOOKS

ISBN: 978 1 85224 887 1

First published 2010 by
Bloodaxe Books Ltd,
Eastburn,
South Park,
Hexham,
Northumberland NE46 1BS.

www.bloodaxebooks.com
For further information about Bloodaxe titles
please visit our website or write to
the above address for a catalogue.

Supported using public funding by
ARTS COUNCIL
ENGLAND

ACKNOWLEDGEMENTS
This book has been published with the generous support
of the Marianne and Marcus Wallenberg Foundation
and with a translation subsidy from the Swedish Arts Council.
Special thanks are also due to Göran Bäckstrand, Kjell Espmark,
Johan Lundberg, Harriet Martinson and Staffan Söderblom.

Cover design: Neil Astley & Pamela Robertson-Pearce.

This is a digital reprint of the 2010 Bloodaxe edition.

CONTENTS

STAFFAN SÖDERBLOM
Reading Harry Martinson

On 6th May 1927, able-seaman Harry Martinson signed off for the last time after seven years on the seven seas. It was his twenty-third birthday and he was returning to his native Sweden to leave behind his life as a stoker and to embark on the life of a writer. All he had by way of formal education was some erratic attendance at rural elementary schools. Two years later he had his first book published, and soon, together with a few like-minded poets and novelists he was making his mark on Swedish literature. His own literary career spanned almost half a century, and in recognition of the extent and influence of his achievement he was awarded the Nobel Prize in Literature in 1974.

1

The approach in Martinson's earlier poetry and prose was something new in Swedish literature, new enough for some readers to find unsettling. A hard life in distant ports and exhausting labour on far away oceans meant that his experience was of a kind which few of his readers felt they had much in common with. His texts were full of exotic geography, rough living and hard-bought knowledge, raw sensitivity – all suggested in shimmering language, swirling light-footed metaphors, deep playfulness. At the same time readers found in his writing images from Swedish nature so finely tuned that their like had not been seen since Linné's observations, two centuries previously. Martinson appeared as the purveyor or interpreter not only of the unknown but also of the intimately familiar, both presented in a poetic language that was felt to be new. The Martinsonian 'smile' soon became a literary concept. But beneath the surface there is often at work an accumulation of significance, as in 'Have you seen a steam collier' in his first volume, *Spökskepp* (Ghost Ships) from 1929.

> Have you seen a steam collier come from a hurricane –
> broken booms, wrenched railings,
> dented, wheezing, done-in –
> and a captain quite hoarse?

Snorting, it ties up at the sunlit quay,
deadbeat, licking its sores,
while the steam in the boiler tubes thins away.

We can see at once that the poem consists of two simple parts: a question in four lines and a kind of answer in three.

'Well, have you seen the steam collier?'

'This is what it looks like.'

It is moreover so packed with concrete details, so rough in a way, that it has the authenticity of the world itself – flaky woodwork, metal, hissing steam. In itself it resembles an object that has been roughly handled: it 'is' its motif. And it is self-confident, self-aware. It doesn't hum and haw about the obvious fact that 'you' ('we') have never seen a steam collier, at least not in this miserable state, and certainly not in any Swedish poem before this one. The poet has knowledge that is not the reader's, he is clear about that and has no intention of pretending otherwise. The poem delivers this knowledge by means of a compact image, without sentimentality or fancifulness, approaching the reader with neither explanations nor adjustments, it is uninterested in poetic diplomacy – it is fundamentally matter-of-fact. The reader's response must then be: no, 'we' haven't seen such a collier. Or: 'we' have now seen the description of the collier, here in the poem – the broken booms, the smashed railings, the dented hull – the ship's lacerated being, which has survived the fury of the elements and can finally come to rest. But the hurricane, the innermost knowledge of the poem, is something we have not experienced, and it is something about which the poem remains silent.

Or have we?

What makes this poem unusual is not that the poet has knowledge of the perils of life at sea, which 'we' for the most part lack. The value of the poem lies not in its information, that it presents a poetic image which we really hadn't previously seen the likes of. The poet certainly indicates a self-conscious frontier between himself and his reader, but Martinson was hardly the kind of poet who sought confrontation for the sake of confrontation. On the contrary, he marks out a boundary in order for it to be crossed, so that 'we' can cross it. He lets the language play its own game, beyond the merely lexical, in the sounds of the poem. The Swedish word for 'steam collier' – *koltramp* – is itself ungainly with its colliding consonants, and the first three lines of the poem bustle with jostling sounds, jolting and rasping consonants played against dark vowels. Non-Swedish readers can observe this by just looking at the text, and Robin Fulton's translation has kept much of the effect. It is in these first lines that the hurricane is perceptible, although it is not described – the thrashing of breakers against the hull, the crunching of woodwork, the giving-way of metal: the reader's journey here is uneasy and tense.

The word-play in the last three lines of the Swedish text, the storm now over, is different: no violent thumps but various hissing consonants and a steadily falling rhythm, like one drawn out exhalation, tension relaxing, relief taking its place, and at last rest.

And this is something which 'we' of course have been through. 'We' too have licked our wounds after turbulent experience, this is something 'we' recognise. The poem carries another narrative within its word-play and it is this other narrative that allows 'us' to step over the knowledge gap between poet and reader – to step over it but not to ignore or forget it. The borderline between the poet's experience and ours remains intact, but is maintained with humility. 'We' read the poem physically, inasmuch as Martinson once experienced it 'in the flesh,' once wrote it with the knowledge and memory of his body. In this way 'we' can become an elementarily human we, without quotation marks – at any rate here, in 'Have you seen a steam collier'.

2

Martinson's poems about Swedish nature distinguish themselves from those based on his experience of life on the oceans. They have a more intimate tone, are sharp of hearing, finely tuned, now and then even devotional. They are anchored in a small-scale pre-industrial peasant landscape, with meadows, pastures, groves of light deciduous trees and dark conifers – sparsely populated, but with an intense presence of singing thrushes and humming insects, and it is nearly always summer. The farmsteads and hamlets all lie at a distance from each other, as in 'Home Village', from *Nomad* (1931), the collection with which his reputation truly began. The poem is about a seaman returning to his home tract in the countryside:

In the gardens of the home village, where earthworms
loosen the soil, the columbine still grows
and grandfather clocks cluck old-fashionedly in each house.
Smoke rises from cottages like sacrificial pillars
and to those who come from afar, from the hard toils
of the world's oceans and the brothel alleys of Barcelona,
this peaceful village is like a silent lie.
A lie one would willingly hang on to, a lie
for which one would trample down all evil truths.

Read hastily, this poem presents a classic confrontation: narrow idyll versus wider world. The picture it gives is of a humble life, more or less at a standstill, furnished with the typical stage-props of the idyllic – cottages, flower beds, wood-burning hearth – everything which in its outmoded and reticent manner speaks of peace and quiet, off the beaten track, a life of poverty and foster care. Every movement, as the poem begins, is slow: that of the worms down in the soil, of the clock pendulum, of the smoke as it rises from the chimneys. There is a deep silence here, only the tick of the clock can be heard. And in contrast to the innocent idyll, we then come to the second half of the poem with 'the hard toils of the world's oceans and the brothel alleys of Barcelona', the world of evil truths.

This is how the poem wants to be read.

But there is also something else at work in its revelation, in the peaceful idyll: an almost imperceptible movement in everything that is still. Something is rising, towering up – a movement that begins down among the worms and rises through the upward-reaching flower, continues in the tall grandfather clock, and soars aloft with the smoke from the chimneys. Among the flower beds and low-lying cottages this movement stretches up, a kind of transparent form, dramatically. The stillness is at once apparent, tense. The home village which appeared to be empty of people in the poem, is at once charged with presence, invisible and therefore threatening – someone is close by, someone who is not showing himself, standing hidden within the idyll and waiting to take a swift step into the picture and transform it.

No one takes that step.

No one reveals himself.

Only the observer is visible, the man from the seas and the hard world, diminishing in the face of this towering movement.

He thinks that the idyll is a lie.

And he thinks that one would willingly 'trample down all evil truths' for the sake of that lie.

Would, willingly.

Why is that not possible?

Perhaps because the evil truths belong precisely here in the rural idyll, at least for the seaman who was Harry Martinson. They exist there, invisible, and as yet undescribed, indescribable. The poem indicates them as a kind of vacant space, something which has been removed, cut away from the picture. The evil truths are perceptible only as an absence.

3

Martinson was born in 1904, in Blekinge, a rural province in the south-east corner of Sweden. He was the only boy among six sisters; their father was a country shopkeeper and their mother had been a housemaid. The parents' marriage was strained and at times violent, and in 1905 the father took himself off to the USA to avoid imprisonment. He came home in 1909 but was again sentenced for violence, and a year later died. In the same year the mother emigrated by herself to the USA, leaving the children behind. She never returned to Sweden and Harry never saw her again. In 1912 he was bound over by the local pauper guardians to a small farmer in the district and in the course of the following four years was placed as a parish orphan with five or six different farmsteads, where he worked as a farmhand and shepherd boy, and in 1916-17 he was housed in a home for elderly paupers. His life was rootless, characterised by abandonment, shame, humiliation, and at times, mistreatment. On repeated occasions he ran away, hoping to reach the port of Gothenburg on the Swedish west coast. In 1920 he signed on for the first time and spent the next seven years as a sailor and wanderer in most corners of the world. After signing off for the last time he lived mostly in Stockholm or in the countryside nearby, as an author.

4

His experiences as a parish orphan living on charity, fatherless and abandoned by his mother – that is the evil truth which in various ways Martinson circled round in his first poetry collections and prose books, up to 1935 when the autobiographical novel *Nässlorna blomma* (Flowering Nettles) was published. It is the story of a homeless boy in early twentieth century rural Sweden, and is now counted among the classic Swedish accounts of childhood. It is written with the same light-footed and playful language as his poetry, as if the blackest of experience can be formulated only in a shimmering, almost weightless prose. *Vägen ut* (The Way Out) came in 1936, following the boy until he stands on the deck of his first vessel, on his way from Gothenburg out into the North Sea. These two novels, or 'documents' as Martinson himself preferred to call them, met with considerable public success, but when he was finished with them his writing entered a kind of crisis.

He deprecated not only his popularity but also the literary means which had brought it about – the playfulness, the metaphors, the smiling images. He demanded of his writing a new clarity, a philosophical seriousness, a linguistic honesty devoid of suggestiveness or seduction. He set aside poetry for a decade and instead wrote prose books of various kinds – observations on nature and the approaching war, polemics against technological uniformity, an account of his short period as a volunteer in the Winter War in Finland in 1940.

It wasn't until 1945 that he returned to poetry with *Passad* (Trade Wind), one of his most important individual books. The subjects are much the same as before, the oceans and the winds, and Swedish nature, but there are also weighty speculative poems, reflecting his insights into contemporary science, or with distinct features of classical Chinese Taoist philosophy. But even if he sought a more direct poetic speech in this volume there is a degree of mysticism still there in his experience of nature, of a sort of eternal cosmic energy that pulses through creation in his texts, but no angels, no divinity. He had a certain religious instinct, but his writing was never confessional. What he called the mystery, or the enigma, reveals itself everywhere in creation, and with its fine awareness and sensitivity his poetry can at times resemble a membrane for this mystery, as in 'Evening Inland':

> Silently the mystery is mirrored. It spins evening
> in quietened reed-beds.
> Here is a gossamer no one notices
> threads from grass to grass.

Silently cattle stare with green eyes.
Soon, evening-calmly, they reach water.
And the lake holds to all mouths
its giant spoon.

The elementary properties are those of so many of his nature poems – pasture land, a lake, grazing cattle, and it's the twilight hour, evening in the simple pastoral. At the same time the poem consists only of reflections, of something which remains invisible: what he calls the enigma.

The poem starts with a moment of absolute stillness, where nothing is really visible, not even the lake where the enigma is mirrored. It is as if the entire attentiveness of the poem is devoted to this very stillness, so that the mirroring of the enigma may be perceived. But as soon as this happens a kind of secret energy becomes active: it spins evening in the reeds which have quietened, spins together creation, a gossamer which no one can see but which everyone is a part of. Everything is part of the web and woof of reflections – the evening, the silence, the reeds, the grass. Everything has its existence in the 'gossamer', fragile, lightly shimmering in the evening. And the poem itself is part of this tissue. The second stanza mirrors the first, the text starts up again, 'silently', and continues into the palpable scene. The cattle, green-eyed, reflect the surrounding vegetation in the same way as the invisible water has just reflected the invisible enigma. As the cattle approach the water 'evening-calmly' they are in tune with the evening, they move down to the lake as if to an elementary sacrament. This is a happening which is repeated and continues, with no beginning and no end, an imperceptible movement in the deep stillness. In the movement the water too "materialises", the enigma's first element, without being trivialised. The poem ends with a metaphor which is not only playful but is also a kind of impossible linguistic formula. The lake can of course resemble a giant spoon, it can indeed be a giant spoon – but no spoon can hold itself. Perhaps that is also how the enigma takes form in the poem, as a hand, invisible but present. This hand in creation is a mystical experience, to which as a reader one might not be certain to subscribe outside the poem. But in the poem's interwoven logic it is incontrovertible.

An extreme mirroring.

The poem as revelation. Or as grace.

5

In 1948 Martinson published a "tramp novel", *Vägen till Klockrike* (The Road to Klockrike), about a group of vagabonds who lack both the will and the ability to adapt to an increasingly industrialised society. They can almost be regarded as a group of Taoist philosophers. He had already told the story of the homeless child who had not chosen to be homeless, and this "tramp novel" can be read as the story of the adult who chooses homelessness, who refuses to conform. Just as *Flowering Nettles* grew from a poetic practice so *The Road to Klockrike* is an application in prose of the poetic approach we find in *Trade Wind*. These two books established Martinson as a leading figure in Swedish literature, and in 1949 he was elected into The Swedish Academy.

6

Looking through his telescope one night in the late summer of 1953 Martinson caught sight of the Andromeda galaxy more clearly than he had ever seen it before. For him this was a revolutionary image of humanity's situation, and in the course of fourteen days in October of that year he dictated, for his wife, 'almost as if under psychoanalysis' the body of texts from which the first twenty-nine songs of the space epic *Aniara* came to be sorted out. These were included in his collection *Cicada* (1953) and the completed epic emerged in 1956, a combination of doomsday vision, science fiction, mysticism, political opposition and much else, the whole often being regarded as his most original production.

Here is Robin Fulton's introductory comment on the work:

> Martinson's 'review of mankind in time and space' consists of 103 'songs' varying in length from a few lines to several pages. The narrative framework is: earth is poisoned by radiation and a fleet of spaceships, each accommodating 8,000 passengers, transport humans either to the 'marshlands' of Venus or to the 'tundra' of Mars. Aniara sets off for Mars but is pushed off course by an asteroid (called Hondo, the name of the Japanese island where the atom bomb was dropped). The spaceship is now aimed at the constellation of Lyra and any change of direction is out of the question.
>
> Mima, at first sight a computer-brain smarter than its

creator, becomes more or less a symbol of communication itself: 'her' vision is relentless and when Dorisburg (the Earth) is blown up the horror of the spectacle is too much for her and her systems collapse. Faced with the results of their own destructiveness and against the backdrop of unceasing emptiness, the humans thus trapped try out every possible way of coping with or hiding from their fate.

This scheme gave Martinson ample scope to explore his critical and often pessimistic view of the way civilisation was going. It also gave scholars, encouraged by various remarks of the poet, to track down symbolic suggestions and distinguish multiple layers of significance in the work. In the reception history of Martinson's work as a whole, the strengths and weaknesses of *Aniara* seem to have played a wider role than might have been expected.

Martinson uses a relatively straightforward language throughout the work and the forms recall those of his early pre-Modernist poetry, some songs being in rhymed quatrains, some in blank verse, some in variations of these.

7

With *Aniara* Martinson had completed the thematic arch of his authorship, the arch of homelessness. He had written three great narratives – of the homelsss child, of the homeless man, and in his space-epic, homeless humanity. This had taken him about twenty-five years. He had completed his story.

Almost the same length of time remained for him as a writer.

If there is one word that can sum up the last decades of Martinson's writing life, it could be: 'loss.' In his poetry of these years he formulated his deepening disquiet about contemporary life: the mechanisation of the landscape, the poisoning of air and water, changes which we now see in terms of climate change, in describing which he was ahead of his time. He was at cross purposes with modernity and the progressive optimism of the early sixties, and what impoverished nature also damaged the very root-system of his own poetic language. In a seminal essay in *Utsikt från en grästuva* (Views from a Tuft of Grass) 1963 he wrote:

> One has to cope with experiences as if one had some kind of inbuilt separator in heart and brain. The senses detach and excuse themselves, the face keeps the right mien in the awful

charade, and a false little piece of natural description emerges. The falsity consists of course mainly in the fact that the real truth about noise, pollution and destruction is stifled into silence. Here you are – a little picture of a peaceful lake.

The only possibility for an authentic poetry of nature was in the memories of the child's self-forgetting play:

> If one played with a dry leaf then the leaf was meaningful just as it was, as a dry leaf with a large number of fine qualities. It could rustle faintly if it was blown along the ground, and if you held it up and let it fall it would drift gently down, swaying to and fro until it reached the grass, only to demonstrate yet another fine property, its lightness and quick readiness to stir, at any moment, in response to the least breath of air. Always it kept itself within the limits of what a dry leaf can manage, and just while the playing child remained like a dry leaf sensitive in eye and imagination and demanded no tremendous or remarkable reason from the leaf, then the dry leaf became almost all-encompassing and could for a few minutes – which because of the intensity of the experience become several centuries – fill the whole of existence with all the meaning required for the occasion.

This is the "parish orphan"s' play, during a couple of moments when no one is watching over him to check that he is doing what he has been told to do, with whatever comes to hand for him who has nothing – the dry leaf. This is a memory free of shame, abandonment, degradation. And it could provide a kind of poetics for Martinson's authorship, for the simple and 'almost all-encompassing' poetry, not least in the last book of poems published in his lifetime, *Tuvor* (Tussocks, 1973). It consists of small poems from Swedish nature, extracts, miniature studies of spruces and birches, doves and thrushes, snails and insects, unassuming motifs. They present a play of language with natural objects, only a few lines at a time, no great secrets to unveil, they exist beyond narratives, beyond categories such as 'light' and 'darkness'. They can remind us of the dry leaf with its fine properties, or, like the ice-age boulder resembling a sideboard in the forest clearing, palpable, incontrovertible, and at the same time impossible to unlock. It preserves its enigma and its integrity.

19

Sideways sunlit
the ground in the clearing is a gold floor
and its grass a sun fleece.
In the midst of this forest chamber
the ancient boulder stands like a sturdy sideboard
with the key turned from inside
and moss in the lock.

8

In 1974 the Swedish Academy awarded the Nobel Prize in Literature to Harry Martinson and Eyvind Johnson. His last years were characterised by illness and withdrawal. After *Tussocks* he wrote nothing more, just sorted out some of the manuscript material he would leave behind and which in due course was published as several posthumous volumes. Harry Martinson died on 11th February 1978.

Translated by Robin Fulton

LIST OF ILLUSTRATIONS

All drawings are by Harry Martinson:

21. From author's manuscript of *Ghost Ships* (1929)
27. The Water-sprite, self-portrait (1930s)
35. Dandelion (date unknown)
49. Carboniferous Age (1941)
61. Woman by the Sea (1939)
79. Cicada (1950s)
97. The Call of Aniara (1950s)
109. Marestail (1930s)
125. Calculation of Uncertainty (1945)
139. Thistle (1938)
153. Back-lit Dandelion with Insects (1930s)

GHOST SHIPS
SPÖKSKEPP
(1929)

The Albatross

Like a messenger of hunger and love
you migrated from
the bay of wind-buoys.
With swishing wingbeats
you raced through the monsoon.
All for the sake of screaming your stormy hunger
for the bird rock Comia
– jutting up stained with breeding places,
gazing out of the West Falklands mists –
and of meeting
an old love-bird from Kamchatka.
You waited for days, then she came
tousled by storms, ruffled by rain
out of a howling easterly.
When the jubilation of breeding had faded
– you storm birds
dived away, sorrowfully screeching, ravenous
back out into the mists of the world.
Albatross and frigate-birds,
you straying children of God's storms.

It's just the kind of day...

It's just the kind of day when we curse shadowless plains.
The stokers roar down there in the heat of hell –
as when you jab a glowing point into crushed ice.
The sea is a swaying fabric of shining oil.
But: a black cloud is swinging its arms over the ocean.
I know: the *Pamperon* will take us –
I saw the wind sow a handful of storm petrels.

Har ni sett en koltramp...

Har ni sett en koltramp komma ur en orkan –
med bräckta bommar, sönderslitna relingar,
bucklig, stånkande, förfelad –
och med en skeppare som är alldeles hes?
Fnysande lägger den till vid den soliga kajen,
utmattad slickande sina sår,
medan ångan tynar i pannorna.

Have you seen a steam collier...

Have you seen a steam collier come from a hurricane –
broken booms, wrenched railings,
dented, wheezing, done-in –
and a captain quite hoarse?
Snorting, it ties up at the sunlit quay,
deadbeat, licking its sores,
while the steam in the boiler tubes thins away.

Dead Seagull

Never again will
my hungry beak spike
the calm of mists.
I'll never again sway
ravenous for fish-oil
on a wave juggling sunlight;
no more on a harsh
skerry gorge myself
on the cod's liver
– never.

But my homeless screech will live in the mist.
You heard it, fisherman,
and the clang of a swaying buoy,
the swell lured you
astray on the sea.
Your rowlocks will never again creak, tugging out there.
– The night is silent –
Long live my desolate cry.

MODERN POETRY
MODERN LYRIK

(1931)

One evening...

One evening in clearest spring
it's so quiet anything could be heard.
On the moor the lapwing's building her rostrum, a criss-cross of twigs.
From there she'll spend three months as the moorland weather sybil
predicting the showers that'll fall on the ploughland's scarecrow
in whose rags the red ants live.
But first she lays on the top three eggs
a little larger than those of a dove.

A bell...

A bell this evening
meanders across the glades –
Mile after mile over the forests: a woodpecker's reverberating hammer.
She wakens a fox
and the moss-clad boulder by the lair's dark eye
glares insidiously in its shadow.
But the sun's lizardy glint can be seen climbing the aspen bole.
While the whortleberry is still young.

Home Village

In the gardens of the home village, where earthworms
loosen the soil, the columbine still grows
and grandfather clocks cluck old-fashionedly in each house.
Smoke rises from cottages like sacrificial pillars
and to those who come from afar, from the hard toils
of the world's oceans and the brothel alleys of Barcelona,
this peaceful village is like a silent lie.
A lie one would willingly hang on to, a lie
for which one would trample down all evil truths.

Cotton

When they'd laid the cable from America to Europe
there was much singing.
The cable, the great singing cable, was put to work
and Europe said to America:
　　Give me three million tons of cotton!

And three million tons of cotton crossed the ocean,
became cloth, to charm Senegambian savages,
became gun-cotton, to slaughter them.

　　Sing high, sing high
　　on every Senegambian sea-route!
　　of cotton!
　　of cotton!

Cotton, cotton, your white snowfall upon the earth!
Your white peace for our shrouds!
Your white top-to-toe robes when we enter heaven
saved by Booth's Jesus-face in all the ports of the world!
　　Cotton, cotton, your snowfall upon the earth!
You fall like the confetti of world events round the machines!

Cable-ship

We fished up the Atlantic cable between Barbados and Tortuga,
held up our lanterns
and patched over the gash on its back,
fifteen degrees north and sixty-one west.
When we put our ears to the gnawed part
we heard the murmuring in the cable.
One of us said: 'It's the millionaires in Montreal and St John's
discussing the price of Cuban sugar
and the lowering of our wages.'

We stood there long, thinking, in a lantern circle,
we patient cable-fishers,
then lowered the mended cable
back to its place in the sea.

Far away from here...

Far away from here I want to send a dream –
high soar the swallows there.
Perhaps your wheat is ripening
and through the yellow oceans of the rye
runs a gentle murmur of bread.
Here is a world of water and stone,
my hand is breadless and I count its lines.

NOMAD
NOMAD
(1931)

Coals

Come down to the trade-winds
and ask us about Durham coals!
Ask us what they're worth
when the barometer plunges like a lightning bolt
and we've got to make it to the Magellan Straits!

Durham coals! These not quite developed diamonds
which an ocean stoker caresses and cherishes
    as if they were breadfruit –
    give us them this day
when devilish Algerian dross smoulders in our furnaces
    and we labour like beasts
when the steam pressure drops on cheerless odysseys.

Don't come with rubies, with blue gleaming jellyfish,
    women's limbs, bread –
but pass us a world's shovel across the sea
    piled with Durham coal!

Come to us, we primitive lovers!
    We primitive lovers of Durham coal.

Out on the Sea

Out on the sea we feel spring or summer only as a breath of wind.
The drifting Florida weed blossoms sometimes in summer,
and on a spring evening a spoonbill flies in towards Holland.

After

After the Battle of Helgoland
and after the Battle of Tsushima
the sea dissolved the driftwood of the human corpses.
Treated them with its secret acids.
Let albatrosses eat their eyes.
And bore them with dissolving salts
slowly back to the ocean –
a creative Cambrian Age water,
to try again.

Asian Tale

In the clenched jaw of the tiger
Karma's son saw a waterlily
and water ran from the whiskers
and the monkeys called: look at that!

Then the waterlily lit up like a spotlight
fumbling over the darkness of the jungle wellspring
and set her pollen on the whisker-stems
and travelled off on the tiger's trail.

She didn't vanish in the great wilds of Asia.
In the liana cables news of her sings
and the monkeys listen; hullo! hullo!
with a spine-chilling roar
she was sown in the north of Burma.

To Be

To be the foster-son of an engine-driver
and travel on an engine festooned with leaves
   all through summer
that's more than God's throne to a youngster on a district line.

Cherry-blossoms rained over us
were sucked into the smoke
and blown up in whirls
like a cloud statue over the Sunday School.
They stuck like God's postage stamps
on each lump of coal in the tender.

Oh those cherry-blossoms that ambushed me
   and my father with beauty
when I was his foster-son for three months!
This memory is dotted by flowers like a bright blouse.
And then that steel beast
which I tamed
and infused with the steam engine's soul!

Cotton-grass

The cotton-grass sways in the evening; tells a riddle:
the swamp rots and dies, the swamp gives back sevenfold.
In the breeze that plays from the pinewood tops
I bow deeply and thank
the slime that fostered my soul.

A Friend's Death

Your journey's over –
they're airing your clothes –
the window's wide open:
on the line a coat with flapping arms
stretches out.
It waves to the rye-stubble,
smells of stable,
is like a suspended past,
a tragedian of the air.
It flaps off, no time to waste,
like the crane, that flies to Africa.

Travelogue

Sought for the purely naked
came to Senegambia –
but cotton cloth was there before me
in stripes and dots and spots
like yellow false snakeskin.

It was only in the brothels the negresses were naked.

But a poor water-girl stood naked one evening
staring in the river.

And there the naked water flowed past
and the naked moon struggled with cloud clothes.
There late at night the woman sang to me
her naked terrible song.

And a hoarse gramophone sang
a foolish ribald refrain
to all the pollen drifting on the trade winds
far out on Cape Verde.

Listener

I was small in the days of listening –
by the hearth sat the old
cradling their supposed sins against
that last day when one
crucified saviour would wash them clean. –

The cat purred, the fire crackled, the flues whistled, –
someone sang downcast and plaintively the song
of the girl who stepped on the bread.
Toothless mouths in late autumns told
of leprous marsh grain and
bitter ergot bloom.
I shivered by my childhood hearth.

Near the Sea

As if endlessly haphazard
the birch forest has pushed its green promontories
into the silent moss
where a hay-barn lies twisted by wind and drought
with a frozen anguish in its wood.

In the all-in-one shadow of the aspens
a horse-drawn rake is sunk
        wheels drowned in grass
and where its long witch-teeth bite the turf
        a pennycress has blossomed.

I have watched a gull come in from the sea
        and perch on the rake seat.
And with that image I have dreamt
        my picture of random happening.

*　*　*

Later poems in this section were added to the 1943 edition of *Nomad*.

Childhood Forest

Barefoot I leapt from tussock to tussock
looking for the farmer's cattle,
saw how the mirrored sky spun
in the pond its wheel of wispy cloud.

It was in the woods of summer where life played,
the evening deep with thrush and the heavens high with swallow.
Nothing came of all my dreams and fablings,
but the memory enlivens my life
and memories are ready-made dreams.

Towards the cowberry distance there
in summer's own parish
my dream migrates
like a crane in spring.

På Kongo

Vårt fartyg 'Havssmedjan' girade ur passaden
och kröp uppåt Kongofloden.
Lianerna hängde nedsläpande på däcken som loggar.
Vi mötte Kongos berömda jättepråmar,
deras heta plåtdäck myllrade av negrer från biflodsområdena.

De satte händerna till munnen
och ropade 'må fan ta dig' på ett bantuspråk.
Vi gledo undrande och beklämda genom tunnlar av grönt
och kocken i sin kabyss tänkte:
'nu skalar jag potatis i det inre av Kongo'.

Om nätterna glodde 'Havssmedjan'
med röda ögon in i djunglerna,
ett djur röt, en djungelråtta plumsade i floden,
en hirsmortel hostade vasst
och en trumma klang dovt någonstans från en by där
gumminegrer levde sitt slavliv.

On the Congo

Our ship *The Sea Forge* swung out of the trade wind
and crept up the Congo River.
The lianas drooped dragging on the deck like log-lines.
We met the Congo's famous iron barges,
their hot plate-decks milling with negroes from the tributaries.

Hands raised to mouths
they called 'Devil take you' in a Bantu tongue.
We slid, wondering and oppressed, through tunnels of greenery
and the cook in his cabin thought:
'Here's me peeling spuds in the Congo interior.'

By night *The Sea Forge* stared
with red eyes into the jungles,
a beast bellowed, a jungle rat plopped in the river,
a millet mortar coughed hoarsely
and a dull drumbeat resounded somewhere from a village
where rubber negroes lived their slave-lives.

Letter from a Cattle-boat

We met Ogden Armour's pleasure yacht
in the latitude of the Balearics.
He is, as is known, our shipowner –
owns five slaughterhouses for pigs in Chicago
and eight for oxen at La Plata.
He put his telescope to his eye and must have said:
– Damn, isn't that my old cattle-boat *Chattanooga*!

We lowered the flag and the oxen took to bellowing
like a thousand hoarse sirens over the endless sea.
It was almost depressing: I felt like
branding everything as the law of the flesh.

After that a heavy storm hit us,
and the oxen, which, as is known, have four stomachs,
suffered dreadfully from seasickness.

NATURE

NATURE

(1934)

Power

The engineer sits by the wheel
reading in the June evening.
The power-station murmurs introvertly in its turbines,
its heart bedded in many layers beats calm and strong.
The leaves don't even tremble
on the big white birch standing shyly by the inlet
    of the concrete dam.
The hedgehog walks along the river-bank munching.
The bridge-keeper's cat listens hungrily to the birdsong.
The lightning-fast power crackles quietly along
hundreds of miles of wire before
breaking into the roar of boastful cities.

The Butterfly

Born to be a butterfly
my cool flame flickers
in the heavy velvet of the grass.
The children chase me. The sun goes down
beyond the mallows and the tussock,
rescuing me till nightfall.
The moon rises: it's far away, I'm not afraid,
I listen to its beams.
My eyes film over protectingly.
My wings are stuck together by dew.
I sit on the nettle.

Argentine Plains

Night drags its rattling mantle along the pampas.
Storms of darkness become storms of daylight in towards the Andes.
The sun rises out of the earth,
looks down on a fleeing cattle herd
    rampaging into the horizons towards Tucumana.
The grass plains thunder beneath the frightened herd,
      their flight roars like a city,
   a whirling city lashed northwards
      by the winds of Tierra del Fuego.

Autumn

The landscape appears with horses
and hard-knuckled ploughmen staring seawards.
The plough makes autumn's first black rip in the yellow stubble
widens its morning wedge to a day's dark rectangle,
bigger and bigger until muffled in dusk,
swelling with its darkness into the night.

Skipper's Ghost

The skipper came home one-legged,
wooden-legged,
filled the doorway
peered in fondly;
from his mouth poured lies,
golden skipper-lies,
he said, with a sneeze:
Salvadorina – well, she was black,
blushing for her
was to be bright as snow in her cheeks,
but a whiter snow you'll hardly find,
you'd have to look in China's porcelain,
in the heart of ivory,
in apple-blossom and milk.
Salvadorina is dead
but lives on in her daughters
and here I go
with my wooden leg full of years
and nails
and arrow dents.
They roasted me whole once,
but the medicine man had helped me with spells;
it was a calf they roasted.
The medicine man got fifteen measures of Inca snuff.
I've got a medal for magic and conjuration.
The years move oddly from west to east.
And you can hear how the deathwatch beetle
ticks in my wooden leg.

Göinge

Between the spruce-boles flies
the wood pigeon's feathered joint.
Above the teeming ant-heap the capercaillie
explodes with its get-away racket.
The swamp's straggling sludge gives way
to the endless goat's hair of purple heather.
Hard as concrete the scoop of the path
holds its course on the millennial heathlands
where poverty-stricken fingers bled
in cleaned-out cowberry twigs.

When credit ran out there remained
the desolate clang of an empty milk churn
the bell of bitterness
in the emigrant's awkward dream
of the West.
The wind sighs now to no one.
The crofts died suddenly among their lilies.
But the chimney walls still wheeze.
And the nettles are in bloom.

The Vision

With scared eyes
the salvation soldiers saw
from the towering helmet of the observatory:
the heavenly harps; the titanic strings of the nebulae,
swaying, chaotic golden gas.

Far out in the immeasurable crystal
of timelessnesses, where terrified thought
can plunge for ever through the millennia,
the golden, gaseous harp-frames stirred
like smoke in Sagittarius.

Ocean Nocturne

Clear winter night,
the stars sparkle coldly;
a boy who longs to go to sea
stands in the still deadly cold with shaking legs
on the bare tabletop of the pier:
he's not counting the stars
but the ships anchored on this earth.
He hears the suspicious shuffle of the watch on deck.

The fleet's funnels
trap starlight in their soot.
Far down the dark anchors sleep;
on dripping chains the starlight climbs aboard
to make off somewhere, to an earthly isle.

Summer Night on the Gulf of Bothnia

Cooled, floated on light, the Bothnian horizon
enters evening's white nothing where each star
is paled by the desolate web of the firmament
and dawn starts where the sun hid itself.

The *Osaka Maru*, far from Nagasaki,
sails up to the light's timberyards at Ume,
tows wondering bushido souls
without lanterns into the shimmer.
And like them others have always wondered;
in a hundred tongues of the sea, asked: why
is the June night so pale on the waves of Bothnia?

The Sea Wind

Over the endless oceans the sea wind sways –
spreads its wings by night and by day,
rises and falls
over the desolate swaying floor of the everlasting oceans.
Dawn is in the offing
nightfall is in the offing
and the sea wind feels on its face – the land wind.

The bell-buoys ring their morning and evening songs,
the smoke of a steamer
or the smoke of Phoenician pitch thins out on the horizons,
a solitary jellyfish sways timelessly to and fro
with shimmering blue roots.
In the offing, nightfall or dawn.

Till Ivar från Harry.

TRADE WIND
PASSAD
(1935)

from **Trade Winds**

I

Where in the realm of symbols can I find
the emblem which may still sustain my journey?
The firm rock is gone – a worn-down ruin,
weathered through the years by knowledge of the roads,
now just mocks the traveller's eye.
Ithaka is gone.

In him, my brother sailor
who keeps himself afloat
while drowned and dead,
symbols still glimmer where he floats in the wave,
like badges stitched in his arm by needles:

the rock with the cross
the shore with the anchor,
the plantain with heart-shaped leaf.

The cross is the cross of the grave,
the anchor has been lowered
to where it can no longer be raised;
the heart-shaped leaf gleams in decay
gilded by sunrise, gilded by sunset.

In seasonless oceans
he is cradled on his way
over the rescue that never was.

On the wide water his body drifts,
far from the uninhabited island
which never
– for him –
turned up to his rescue.
Robinson is gone.

IV

But in their youth beyond Cape Verde
the sailors strode out.

Clad in the sail of the trade wind
they strode on the trade wind paths
out to the sun's altar.

There they listened to the winds talk
not of calm, not of storm, but of eternal freshness –
the trade wind's mighty airing through world and spirit.

The sun, the eternal, crowned the steadfast trade wind with its glow.
The sun was the crown of life.

VI

Who remembers the name of Sebastian de Cano?
Year after year he brought in cargoes of spice
to Lisbon from the Molucca Islands.
He knew Bremen's key, the sea of trade.
With skipper Da Gama he was on hand
when the world grew wider everywhere.
Turmeric, pepper, cassia, cinnamon,
and sandalwood for the king's panelling,
he brought them all from Isla de Susanna.
  His hair turned white as salt
  and his forehead crimson.
  On his flute of cinnamon bark he played
of the seas' time, of the seas' Ispahan.

VIII

The Iberians called the trade wind route the Sea of the Ladies:
el Golfo de las Damas.
They took the ladies out there to dance.
That's how they sailed to the New World.

Their ships had grand names.
Names of an age intoxicated by the sea:
Nuestra Señora de la Encarnacion Desengana.
Nuestra Madre del caba Donga.

And they bowed to their ships as if to ladies
on the world's dance floor,
on el Golfo de las Damas.
And they took them out to dance on the Antillean route, the road
    of the trade wind.

IX

The newly discovered islands multiplied.
Now there are no more undiscovered islands.

Where does the sea go now, still ready
with steadfast driving winds
on the windy path of the Antilles?

Raised on the wings of comfort by the djinns of speed
more and more will look down on the seas of conquered distance.

And the world will slowly lose itself
when it deprives itself
of the strength of desolation
and the adventure of desolation.

All that was remote
will be easily come by and worn down.
The exotic will sink and die
like a final Atlantis,
like a submerged Gondwanaland.

People will call then for a lost distance.
They will call for new worlds.
They will call for a Virginia of the stars.
But bound to the earth they will fly in circles
like birds who have lost their Nile in the heart of Africa,
    their reed-dense remote Siberian marshland by the Yenisei.

Kväll i inlandet

Tyst gåtan speglas. Den spinner afton
i stillnad säv.
Här finns en skirhet som ingen märker
i gräsets väv.

Tyst boskap stirrar med gröna ögon.
Den vandrar kvällslugn till vattnet ned.
Och insjön håller till alla munnar
sin jättesked.

Evening Inland

Silently the mystery is mirrored. It spins evening
in quietened reed-beds.
Here is a gossamer no one notices
threads from grass to grass.

Silently cattle stare with green eyes.
Soon, evening-calmly, they reach water.
And the lake holds to all mouths
its giant spoon.

Moon Poem

The only way out for the dreams,
the moon strip away from land,
sank one morning silent and scared
in the cold sea of want.

This moon path of glittering silver
which he had sat by with her so often
rests now heavy as gravel
on the sea bed off Pater Noster.

The cottage turns grey like their hair
in the sea's inexhaustible winds.
Wide storms all the way from the Orkneys
sweep the churchyard.

The Juniper Bush

He stands silent by the stone,
agrees with the heather.
Among the sharp needles
the berries sit in clusters
like intercepted shotgun pellets.
Nothing gets its teeth into him.
He'll brush the north wind.
His twigs are tough as tendons.
When things are barest, he is most hardy.
Yet still gives a scent, still has charm.
For graves and floors he gave sprigs,
and he brewed a good beer
where he stood, strong and friendly,
clamped between grey stones in Thule.

from Leaves

5

Summer is late and who will praise autumn.
A dying bee whose vigour is fading
stings you as if in sleep.

You feel the wounded tiredness in its sting.
It reaches you like a faint electric signal
           from a cooling earth.

The aspen shakes itself more and more in the wind
and busily hush-hushies at all free birds.

Now and then the whole tree flounces
like a rooster in its years of feebleness.

6

August died, and September
and the glow-worms snuffled out in the chill rains.
Then the frost came: it came early,
and only the stars shone
from on high where no rain storm drenches.

The Midge-catcher

Deep in the pale summer night
the bat circled wildly
in a soundless furioso.
Cut sideways through the mist
like half of a tiny black umbrella
then opened out and hovered.
Next moment
flapped
and ran
on wing hooks helter skelter
like insect legs on the mist.
Hovered again
vanished between spruce trees
came back
and dived
sliced through the singing of the midges
which rose to a whine.

Then I remembered bygone years. An evening with Desdie.
Stars shone cleanly.
She slipped along a path and met me
and my heart thumped
and the bats swooped in Louisiana.

Prodigal Son

The prodigal son came home.
There was fatted calf for dinner.
The father sat there with his huge coal-black beard from Babylon.
There were things he wanted to ask about
but they no longer spoke the same language,
besides he didn't want to make a fool of himself.
They ate in silence.
The son was hungrier than he wished to show.
The platter of fatted calf was passed round several times
and all of them in fact had a good appetite.
I want to tell you, said the lost son,
but a crumb stuck in his throat and he had to cough,
after which he forgot what he had to say and went on eating.
The meal over, the mother washed up.
She was tearful and stooped.
The son lay down outside in the grass and looked up at the clouds
and the father went and broodingly combed that Babylonian beard.

The Cockchafers

The summer evening is pale like the white of a beautiful eye.
The cockchafers pass
with a dull drawn-out droning.

When at some point they land
you can see their old-fashioned splendour,
the dulled green-golden shimmer of the wing sheaths
like that of Indian brass.

Picture by Water

The watery forest of the reeds
rustles with countless pennants.
The crown of an aspen trembles
and its eager leaf-whisperings
spill out in an invisible swarm towards the islet.
A woman is seen bathing.
A grebe swims off.
He twists his head almost right round.
It's like a colourful weathervane.

In June

Spring's last stars show up but lack sharpness.
They are small, moon-pale, stingless.
Tired of glittering in the winters
they rest in the brightness of summer nights.

Hades and Euclid

I

When Euclid set out to measure Hades
he found it lacked depth and height.
Demons flatter than skate fish
rampaged on the plains of death,
scuttled barking without echo
along fire lines and ice lines,
along the drawn lines of Hades.

Alongside lines that broke
but joined into lines again
line-swarm after line-swarm thronged,
demons abreast, in line, in parallel through Hades.

Waves there were none, no heights, no deeps, no dales.
Only lines, parallel courses, two-dimensional angles.
Demons moved like elliptical plates;
carpeted endless ground as if with wandering dragonscales in Hades.

On levelled burial sites where oblivion ravaged with its flatness
snakes crawled – themselves just rougher lines:
raced, squirmed, stung
along running lines.

A roaring grass-blaze in a furious stampede
skimmed over the ground like a carpenter's plane of fire.
It bulldozed across evil prairies, evil steppes, flat evil pustas,
to and fro, endlessly reignited
by the heat of the flat plains of Hades.

II

Hell's ovens lay low
on the flat plain.
There, in brick ovens
– superficially like the graves of the dead –

they burned the fortuitously judged,
the victims of flat evil,
no comfort from a height
no support from a depth,
treated without dignity,
treated without stature,
treated without the moderation of eternity.
Their lamentations were met with mockery
on the flat plain of evil.

And Euclid, king of moderation, wept
and his cries sought out the god of the sphere,
the son of Kronos.

III

That was Hades.
Searching glances roved
but found no
standing forest
rustling tree-tops.
No bird rose,
no fish of the deeps
sought the peace of a sea bed.
No one lowered
sinker or net in the depths.
No one went down or came up.

All raged, all sorrowed, all laughed, hated, took revenge
trapped in the line, in the surface
in the endless flatness
in the evil web.

That was Hades, the flatland of evil,
battlefield of ravaging, plain of revenge.
The light of the sun rebounded there,
turned into cold glitter from an evil mirror:
the mirror of empty delusions.
No stone there was left on stone.

That was Hades
where life edged forward
to avoid falling
to lead rain, steel rain, copper rain
storming densely
along the ground in Hades.

And Euclid stumbled face down.
The great measurer pressed himself to the ground,
bit into its soil and wept.

He cried:
Who climbs up?
Who climbs down?
Who climbs up with good will?
Who climbs down in the depths
with the searching eye and the heart of truth?

He listened with his ear to the ground.
He listened for long as if on a burning prairie
with his ear to the ground.

He listened for a thousand years. He listened for another thousand.
And at last he heard.
He heard a sea.
He heard a well-spring ripple.
He heard how the grass grew.
He heard a world's spring, a summer of ripening.
He heard a wisdom that blew clean.
It had a scent of fruit and the sea,
it had the scent of Arcadia.

And he heard of good will a wave
through everyone
through all peoples.
He heard a high and deep current,
a steady and high trade wind.

It came to freshen,
it came to awake.

It came to refresh
to ripeness and growth, to high and deep,
to the lush realm of a good will to all
that surface which so terrified him,
that surface which so plagued him for a thousand years
and then for a thousand more:
that surface raging in Hades.

Duvkullorna

Skogsstjärnorna frodas aldrig.
De bara reder sig
med karg nätthet i mossan.

De är spensliga,
men veta ingenting om den söta vekhet
du vill tillskylla sommaren.
Det spensligas bestämdhet
är inte mindre än ekens.

Chickweed Wintergreen

Never luxuriates.
Yet manages, sparingly
and neatly in the moss.

The flowers are delicate
but know nothing of the sweet pliancy
you would foist on summer.
The determination of the fragile
is no less than that of the oak.

CICADA
CIKADA
(1953)

Extinction

Turning his back on the days of men, Tycho Brahe gazed
at a cosmos where the faces of suns blaze.
One night as a nova burned itself out, a sun in collapse,
he heard behind him a lamenting workaday woman:

'Merciful Lord, my child is failing.
By sunrise my boy will be dead.'

Tycho stood unmoving and watched the nova in his telescope,
observed how a sun went down for good on worlds enjoying its
          favour,
considered the inhabitants of these worlds, their kingdoms caught
          unawares,
all they had dealt in, dreamt and known
by the date the flame burst
suddenly from white-hot heavens
the oceans of worlds were too puny to quench.

He shivered and felt the nameless pain from Cassiopeia,
and without turning to her said to the grieving woman:
'Woman, you mentioned the sun. You remembered it existed.
Your powers of memory are great.
How is your boy? Is he ill?'

Winter Dream

Dreamt I was a black man.
Trapped in
by all the mighty whiteness
its hostile winter wood:
the galloping clan
of snow-heavy spruce.
They came in their thousands, in conical snow capes,
crowded in closer, heavier and whiter,
clenched me in the clearing,
tarred me on the roadway,
rolled me on the ridge
in the snowy winter's froth of feathers.
Their laughter was raucous as I groped blindly
and hobbled away greased in degradation
along the trampled, unravelling track.
And the echo of white voices
and the echo of white hills, booming
when everyone shrieked in my tarred ear:
'Isn't it fun to be alive?
Look around you, the world's full of winter!'

The Fascination of Speed

Complain they well may, the flowers and foliage here
which mere chance allotted
to the broad verge of dust.
They live in dust land, a dust corridor
all summers long
in the wheel-spun dust cyclones.

There's no stopping the vehicles rushing past
and grass and cow-parsley shrink more and more
beneath the degradation of dust.
Each leaf is like an outstretched cracked tongue
coated with grey powder.

What a dry as dust image
of mankind's trail of drought and death:
this broom of dust
sweeping the forests with dust.
If trees could shy away from men
the forest would be desert.

Swedish Folktale

He desired her all the way through the mountain.
But the conditions laid down made a new mountain.
First he must break up all of winter's ice
as far as the sowing grounds of spring.
Then he must hack his way through spring's thickets
as far as rapturous summer woods.
There he can meet her.
But their meeting was so shy it could only be brusque,
tenderness so feeble it was all heavy-handed.
The soft word was a self-contradiction, like rowanberry honey.
And so began their life together.
They pushed into the everyday laborious grey mountain.
The mountain closed round them for good.
For a few years cries could be heard from inside,
hammer-blows for many years, they wanted out, they wanted out.
But in due course even the hammer-blows fell silent.
The grey mountain lay there soundless and mighty,
and the winters snowed down.

Mouldering Cottage

The white cow-parsley with its gossamer blossoms
came to be the last curtains of the abandoned cottage.
The broken-backed roof has collapsed into the house.
The path is only a grassy strip, untrodden now.
But the juniper bush and the stone have moved closer together.
They are getting married, in a hundred years.

Crab Apple Tree

Looks despised down in the water,
sees its yellow leaves.
Shakes its fruit into the spring
makes an apple soup.
Lives where it is
with the free hard fate of its kind.
Feels freer
than the Tree of Paradise.

Thrall Woman

She tossed her hoe aside
and went up to him saying:
'Don't waste too many years
on the stone of your stubbornness that no one can budge.
Linger now and then with my heart in the dew
and listen to thrush and cuckoo.
The evening sun going down will soon find us old enough
to keep it company forever behind the ridge.'

Japansk målning
Maruyama

En spenslig bro på höga styltor vajar.
Dess bambu knäar till när bonden går.
En snövit hästsvans hänger långt i fjärran.
Det är ett vattenfall i Sugibergen.

Japanese Painting
Maruyama

A slender bridge floats on tall stilts.
Its bamboo knees bend when the peasant crosses.
A snow-white horse-tail hangs far in the distance.
It's a waterfall in the Sugi Hills.

Tropical Myth

The rain cast its net over the forest,
trapped the demon of drought.
Lightning held its lantern high,
it flickered, quenched, flared again
till all was over and the trees shook off their wetness.
Everything was clear again.
The apes wove
the rising moon
into a thin basket of lianas.
The moon escaped
but lost its glow
on the black howler monkey
and the branches of the mohra tree.
That's how fireflies began.

The Islet

The grebe twists its head, turns
plunges its neck like a bright arrow
and the water rings widen.
 The islet sways
glides forward like a ship with a rigging of oaks,
plays for a while with its centuries in the wave of the moment.

The Cuckoo

Spring can be heard in the woods
and everyone called Otto
thinks the cuckoo is calling him.
But the cuckoo is just holding an auction
on his own bankruptcy estate.
He's about to farm out his own son.

The Swan

The swan makes a greedy swipe
with his white hook of a neck,
hacks with a sideways sickle
in the forest of pondweed.
Bores with his awl of a beak
in the slime's rotten velvet,
raises his head and glares
snaky-cold around the bay of dreams.

After Dew-fall

An orchid-hunting moth
waves with silent wings in the dusk of grass
and the snail emerges deep black,
starts his trudge in the direction of the mist.
It is all so still not even grass blades have the heart to stir.
But suddenly and soundlessly
night starts by tossing
its glove through the midge-cloud:
a bat.

Forest Poem

The sun leaves the forest
through the most westerly clearing
and the mountain starts to cool.
A song-thrush tries to explain what's happening
but the stock dove works up a fit of grief.
She moans dully and at length like a widow.
She points with a wing towards the moor
where the sun gently sinks as if in a quagmire.

Remote

Close by the forest lake
wreathed by bog myrtle, abandoned,
the outlying barn stands
empty, lopsided as a wood-shaving basket.
And down by the shore the wave licks
with a black and greedy tongue of mud
a cracked and vainly tarred boat.

I Love Driftwood

I love driftwood
from far away.
North Atlantic wood, turned, drenched and shaped
by the sea's lathes
in the swell on desolate coasts,
the organ-pipes of ice off Labrador.

I seek out company, feeling weak and lost
and in terror of dumb forces.

But if I were made
with strength enough to survive
as seals do on the ocean of loneliness
I would at last die solitary
as only driftwood drifts
and is gurgled and ground into the sea
the organ-pipes of ice off Labrador.

Meek

People got worked up at the old miller
because of the moss on his mill wheel.
They called it the weeds of decay.

The old miller let them be.
He thought: I'll soon be at rest in my grave anyway.
And each generation has its own moss
which at last, like me, it finds no point in defending,
for each generation starts its course
with blindness backwards and wolfish greed forwards
and ends its course with longing backwards where life was
and hatred aimed ahead where death is.
Otherwise he could have told them
that moss on a wooden mill wheel
is a good cure against drying-out and creaking.

So simple it can be
with everything one silently knows about
but finds it pointless to talk about.

A completely moss-free and bare water wheel
crumbles away faster in summer.

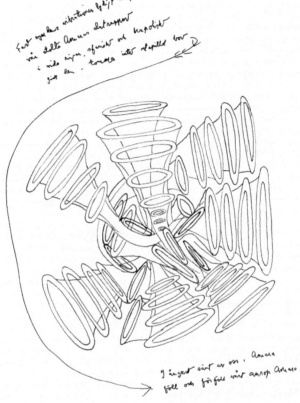

ANIARA
ANIARA
(1956)

from **13**

Year six and *Aniara* still on course
for Lyra, still with undiminished speed.
Holding up a handsome bowl of glass,
the chief astronomer set out for us
– the emigrants – his current views on space:

'We're starting slowly to suspect these depths
we're hurtling through are of another kind
than what we thought each time the concept "space"
on Earth inspired imaginative flights.
We're starting to suspect our loss of way
is much more drastic than we first assumed.
Our knowledge is perhaps naivety
which based on narrow-minded evidence
concluded that the Riddle has design.
We're close to thinking now that all this space
and glass-like clarity around our hull
is spirit everlasting, out of grasp,
the spirit's ocean where we've lost our course.
Our spaceship *Aniara* hurtles on
through something where the working of a brain
fulfils no need: there are no brain cells here.
It's spirit, greater than the world of thought.
Through God and Death and Things Ineffable
our spaceship *Aniara* hurtles on.
We have no destination, leave no wake.

If only we could turn, go back to base
now that we have discovered what our ship
in essence is: a tiny bubble locked
in glass, in glass of God's own spirit locked.

I'll tell you what I heard of glass: you'll see
then what I mean. In every piece that's left
untouched for long enough its bubble moves
interminably slowly to a new

98

position in the body of the glass
so after gradual millennia
the speck of air has journeyed through its glass.

The same way in interminable space
abyss within abyss where light-years plunge
around the bubble *Aniara* is.
For though the speed with which she flies is great
– she'd leave the swiftest planet far behind –
yet seen against the depths of space her speed
exactly matches that with which we know
the bubble makes its journey through its glass.'

from **26**

Deaf-and-dumb he started to describe
the worst sound he'd heard. It wasn't heard.
Just when the ear's membranes burst
there came like a whoosh through melancholy reeds the last –
when that phototurb crushed Dorisburg.
It wasn't heard, the deaf man concluded.
My ear couldn't keep up
when the soul was blown to pieces,
when the body was thrown to pieces
when built-up square-miles wrenched
themselves outside-in
when that explosion crushed
the great city called Dorisburg.

So spoke the deaf man who was dead.
But as it was said that stones would cry out
so spoke the dead man in a stone.
He cried out of the stone: can you hear.
He cried out of the stone: can't you hear.
I come from the city of Dorisburg.

Then the blind man began to tell
of the gruesome piercing glare
that dazzled him.
He wasn't able to describe it.
But gave one detail: he saw with the back of his head.

His whole skull became an eye
dazzled beyond the tolerance of blast
lifted and carried off in blind trust
in the sleep of death. But sleep there was none.

In that the blind man resembles the deaf man.
And as it was said that stones would cry out
so he cries out of stones with the deaf man.
So they both cry out of stones with each other.

So they both cry out of stones with Cassandra.

To mima I rush as if I could
check the terrible deed in my alarm.
But mima shows it all, implacable, clear –
fire and death to the very last image
and turning to the passengers I cry
the pain of my pain at the death of Doris:

Defence is possible against almost
anything, fire, ravages of storm and cold
– count up what catastrophes you can.
But no defence is possible against man.

– – –

The blue lightning strikes mima blind
and I lose all words for what overcomes
the poor Earth, all the way here that flash
blasts into my heart, an open gash.
And I the faithful mima's faithful ministrant
in iced blood the evil message find
that Doris died in distant Dorisburg.

from **49**

This long road I now have travelled
from Rind to here
is night-coloured like the road
I walked in Rind.
Dark as before. As always.
The darkness, though, grew chill.
And that's the difference.
Endurable darkness abandoned me
and to my temples
and to my breast that belonged to spring
the cold darkness came and stayed
for always.
A desolate rustling from the aspens in Rind
rattled in the night. I began to freeze.
That was in autumn. They talked about the glow of maples.
And passers-by I heard praise
the sunset in a local valley.
It was described as red
with bright spokes and evening purple.
And just opposite, it was said, the wood
flared in the last light.
It was mentioned also how the shade beneath the trees
as the frost came turned white
as if its grass were summer's hair
quickly ageing.
That's how the scene was told to me:
new frost white on gold that glowed
when summer paid what it owed
to its debt-collector – cold.
And autumn's great squandering was told too,
everything golden thrown in summer's grave.
Such splendour on display
like a gypsy funeral they said,
all the glad-rags, the yellow, the red,
and golden banners from Ispahan.

But there I stood in darkness, speechless, cold
just hearing how everything I held dear
vanished in a dark and icy wind
and the aspen's final trembling told me how
summer would soon die in the land of Rind.

Then the wind swung round
and in the night
the terrifying black heat arrived.
I fell into the arms of someone who came running
and that someone frightened me.
How could I know in that hot darkness who
it was
that caught me as I fell and held me fast.
He might have been a devil or a human.
As the thundering grew louder, the hot blast
became a hurricane
and he who held me shouted louder louder
in a voice that still seemed far away:
shield your eyes. It's coming. You'll be blinded.
I made my voice as shrill as possible
and shrieked back: I am blind
and so am shielded. I have never seen,
but always knew by touch the land of Rind.

He let me go and ran to save his life,
I don't know where in the scorching din of darkness
which could suddenly be overcome only
by frightful peals of thunder from far away
rolling towards me who was blind.
Down I fell again, began to crawl.
I crept in the woods in the land of Rind.

I managed to reach a stony hollow where
the trees didn't fall and the heat wasn't hard.
I lay there almost happy among the stones
and prayed to the god Rind for help and succour.
And someone stepped in from the tempest
(a miracle)

and bore me to a carriage with drawn blinds
and someone drove me through the night
to Rindon's field
where someone from the refugee camp
voiceless from shouting hoarsely hissed
my number and my name and sent me with
the crowd streaming to the goldonder sluice.

The years that followed then became my fate.
I learned on the Martian tundra how
like a messenger from Rind to move the guards
with lamentations on fate's hard blows.
I learned the braille of the great scream
in the faces I felt over with my hand.
It was as the Singer of Save the Tundra
I then came back to my own land.

There all was cold now. All growth was stunted.
By sheer will-power they carried out their plan
to try to save the soil with a substance
the scientists had come up with: geosan.
How it worked out I can't explain
and many said it couldn't help.
'What no one could but everyone desired'
was how the plan was commonly described.
And then I left both my home and the source
of songs about the land of Rind and sought
a place as singer in the Third Hall.
There I am now and sing 'Oh that vale'
and 'Little bird out in the rose thickets'.
But also 'The Cast-Iron Ballad', that gonders
sing so often in our goldonder.

In our eleventh year we saw a vision,
the slenderest of visions, the most meagre –
a spear travelling the Universe.
It came from where our space-ship came
and held its course, undeviating.
Its speed being greater than *Aniara*'s
meant it drew ahead and left us.

But afterwards we sat for long in groups
eagerly deliberating what
the spear could be, its course, its origin.
No one knew and no one could have known.
Some guessed but no one was convinced.
It was in some way not to be believed,
was pointless as an object of belief.
It just – flew across the Universe.
The spear of emptiness made its way
pointlessly. Yet that vision
had the power to touch the brains of many.
Three went mad, one committed suicide.
And still another founded a new sect,
a shrilly dry, ascetically boring crowd
who made their presence felt among us long and loud.

That spear then had as good as struck us all.

from **72**

The time passed the years flowed away in cold hard space.
Life became more and more timeless for most, sitting
staring out of wide windows, waiting for some star
to separate from the others, come our way, come close.

Children grew up and played on the tundras of the imprisoned,
on the worn ballroom floors more and more pitted and scraped.
New times new customs, old dances long forgotten
and dance-crazed Daisy slept for ever in her shell
in the vault where only queens of the dancefloor slept.

I sat in silence dreamt of glorious Karelia
where once I lived, where once I spent a lifetime
stayed for thirty ample winters and for nine and twenty summers
before I once again tried other countries, other destinies
on my slow-moving transmigration.

Memory comes back in glints. Here in space there's no hindrance,
times stream together, I recall from different lands
fragments of my long pilgrimage.
Most beautiful among the beautiful, glimpses of Karelia still shine
like a glint of water through the trees, like a brightening lake in
        summer

in the whiteness of June when evening scarcely dims
before the flute-clear cuckoo calls sweet Aino
to bring the veil of mist with her, to rise from lakes of June
walk to the rising smoke, come to hear the joyful cuckoo
in rustling Karelia.

103

Jag skruvar lampan ner och bjuder frid.
Vårt sorgespel är slut. Jag återgav
med sändebudets rätt från tid till tid
vårt öde speglat i galaxens hav.

Med oförminskad fart mot Lyrans bild
i femton tusen år goldondern drog
likt ett museum fyllt av ting och ben
och torra växter ifrån Doris skog.

Bisatta i vår stora sarkofag
vi fördes vidare i öde hav
där rymdens natt oändligt skild från dag
en glasklar tystnad välvde kring vår grav.

Vid mimans gravplats stupade i ring
till skuldfri mull förvandlade vi låg
förlossade från bittra stjärnors sting.
Och genom alla drog Nirvanas våg.

103

I bid repose and now turn down my lamp.
Our tragedy is done. I was to tell,
with emissary's right, from time to time
our fate reflected on galactic swell.

To distant Lyra for fifteen thousand years
with unrelenting speed our ship would steer,
a museum, bits and bones stacked on tiers,
and pressed plants from our far-off native sphere.

Laid out and cold in our sarcophagus
we'd sail on desolation's endless wave
the night of space forever lost to day
a glassy silence wrapped around our grave.

By mima's burial place set in a ring
we lay transformed, now guiltless mould
redeemed from bitterness of stars that sting.
And through us all Nirvana's billow rolled.

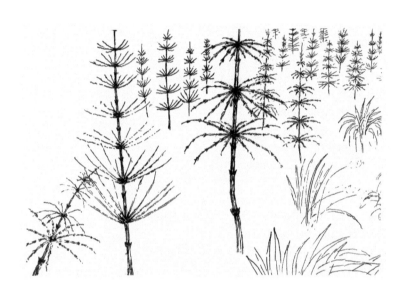

THE GRASS IN THULE
GRÄSEN I THULE
(1958)

The Sand

We watch a human head being prepared:
a sand-hand fills the skull with sand
which is heated up and poured in
then poured out.
And the next hand comes with sand.

The dry sand soon does its job.
In a few days the skull shrinks.
And look where the brain was, each cranny
dried up by the doubt-dry sand
and the skull contracted
smoked-in and ready
for the shelf in the hut.
The head-hunter's triumph.

There is a doubt drier than sand.
There is a sand of doubt afflicting everything.
There is a parcher of souls
with handshake of brick and breath of dust.
There is a dew-drier of song.
There is a desert people who themselves are sand.

The Last Year

That was the year the deserted cottage
in the forest was sold off for firewood.
The demolition men brought their lorry
pulled the place down in three and a quarter hours
and even took away the well-trough.
It wasn't so big once ripped from the well.
They didn't even bother to break it up
but threw it on the platform as it was.
It sat there like a little grey chest, mossed over.

When silence had returned
the weasel crept from the old hearth wall.
She summoned a cuckoo from the forest
and they held a service together.
The cuckoo hooted a cuckoo-hymn.
And that was it. Over.
After that nothing was as it used to be.
But the summers came wandering along
allowing bentgrass and garlands to grow.

The Smith and the Anvil

He knows his anvil. Senses where it takes the blows.
Its massiveness shivered through by boom waves from hammer thuds.
In its braced iron body rings widen as in water.
Scarcely yielding it thrusts back a reply to everything worth a reply.

Assurbanipal's Slave

Being a slave under The Great King Assurbanipal
Lord of the World
was better than being his adviser or his vassal-king.
The post of adviser especially was unsafe.
The Great King's wrath was that of the lion ripping its prey.
Many advisers were flayed.
The slave's service however was tolerable, on account of
    The Great King's decree
that slaves, horses and hounds should be treated equally
and be well-maintained and with happy eyes while
    on palace duty.
This decree being consistently observed
and the slaves themselves presenting a well groomed
    appearance,
I survived, as a slave, many good advisers.
Not even the wily Kadsebuk
– well versed in the wrath of lions –
managed to outlive me.
His skin was stretched on the Wall of Wrath
while mine was oiled daily for guard duty.
I belonged to The Fragrant Watch.
Each day at the hour of washing
I was tended and fussed over
with the same scrutiny as if I were a hunting steed or palace poodle.
In this way I could live my years
while many others, highly placed,
like ministering moths
were incinerated by The Great King,
Lamp of Lamps.

The Bat

Soundlessly in bravado sweeps
the bat hurls himself.
Too swift for anyone to see
the little flattened face
silently gathers the midges in its leather pouch.
Having accumulated enough to be sated upon
it hangs itself up with all it owns
folded together beneath the rafter.

Li Ti's Advice

If you own two coins, said Li Ti on a journey,
buy a loaf and a flower.
The loaf's purpose is to feed you.
The flower you buy means
that life is worth living.

Two Japanese Landscapes
Hokusai

1

A farm-house squats in the grass
and over the fields the moon rises.
High on a leaf a cricket giggles.
Then the Yodogawa River sparkles.

2

A cloud has paused above the valley.
A girl glances up at it and calls:
It's the holy bird Kowo
that laid its egg. Now it'll be summer.

The Dragonflies

We have fixed the dragonfly's short life
in a few phrases and proverbs
and mention it sometimes in winter.

The gods will do the same with us one day
when the faint rippling of our rage
has faded out in the Milky Way...

The Cemetery

The leafy groves enclose the cemetery.
In summer's soft voice they spell out
what cannot be called back.
In the grass the wind looks for something lost.
But time has walked out
through the gates of iron.

Summer Going Chill

The wind begins to barge through the autumn of the oaks.
Coolness is gradually infected by coldness.
The shade which just now was comfortable
can no longer befriend those on the road.

The Forest Spring

The forest spring
which keeps hidden among ferns
asks the moon if he
can't stay a while in the round mirror.
But the moon unfortunately must be off
to help out at a party.
He mentions a name with his squint mouth
but just then the woods rustle.

Picasso Painting

A cool weighing up. Well applied tensions.
Demon-balance between blood surfaces and flesh slices.
A few live coals
laid out on vampire velvet.
The world breakfast extra-bold-type newspaper
with double spread death parts
and cleft life parts.
At last a smallish human heart in cross-section
inside an iron stove.

Lacking Strength

In a forest once I found an axe struck into the ground
wedged right in.
As if someone had wanted to split the earth in two
with one blow.
The will had not been lacking, but the handle
broke.

The Breaker

The ice breaker in Thule ploughs full-roar-ahead.
Heaves with creakings and boomings
the white doors heavier than Egypt's
and gargles with floundering snow.

The channel it splits open
becomes a dead-straight prairie road
for the wagons of commerce
in the hard seas of Northern Bothnia.

The Sun

The sun is a hot jewel
never content with its heat and glitter.
Blazing impatiently it throws lightning
at God its Goldsmith.

THE CARRIAGE
VAGNEN
(1960)

Conversation at Dusk

What came of the woman
who rowed in a deep blue blouse
and a cotton skirt of poppy red.

Back she came, in a tarred skiff
clad in widow's black.
Thirty years have gone, she said,
the days of my youth met
an abrupt end one night.
The urge that accompanies all life
also tore a piece out of her heart.
Saying-nothing held out
until it screamed at its own roof.
Hate is an old acquaintance
in the groves of love.

Folktale Heaven

The night-wind sweeps folk-tale heavens together,
moon-silvered clouds.
Curly and seven leagues long.
Many old books open now their little treasure boxes.
Everything is unreasonable and familiar.
Walk over to the hill in the forest.
Read yourself away to these clouds while there is time.

A Thing among Things

Now and then I wanted to be a thing among things.
Was there, in dreams, quite often.
In one, was a water-barrel by the drainpipe,
always running over
unfailingly filled up again
exposed all the time to wind-torn waterfalls
from a gossipy metal lip,
administered disintegrating pine-needles
and sodden leaves from roofs.

Once I was a hoe
thrust nose down in earth,
hauled backwards by the peasant woman.

Just as in ancient tales.
Just as in deeper memories.
A kind of presence
down in the wells.

The Oak's Memory

The highway with its milestone right under my branches.
But I prefer her to come to mind.
She was beautiful on the path.
She came, at least once a century.
Was sometimes away, deeply asleep down in the earth
but rose again so like herself it was her again.
It must have happened in the village
that she woke up anew.
She must have gone back there under the earth.
Overcame, always.
My high branches rustle about her.
I have known her now for seven centuries.
It's still as if last spring.

The Shadows

Since the sap counted the possible growth rings
a sorrow drew a stroke of its bow through the world.
Shadows which belonged here beneath the trees
refused to let themselves fade.
They grew into the ground and stayed there
where the apples had stood
in darkened grass.

Remote Old Farmyard

Apples over-ripened on the tree
remember through sap legends
the girl who plucked apples in autumn,
who for a hundred years
has rested sunk in her grave.

The wooden bucket has a hidden mouth
carved long ago in its base.
It lowers itself in the depth of the well
as far as her youth.
Calls to her,
but she answers only faintly
as if through water.

Wind of Resemblances

To be alive, everything must resemble something.
This is language in motion, sweeping over things.
There is a wind of resemblances.
It freshens, gathers together, separates.
Take it away and you cement the world, become thrall to facts.

In the Reign of the Pharaoh Totmes

Our overseer of the rowers is going to die soon.
Although the voyage has been long he uses the leather scourge
on our gashes and chafed sores.
He takes a beaker of fermented slave-woman's milk at the overseer's
    table.

He is going to die in Dendera. We rowers have decided.
Since we will have killed him, we will all be beheaded on the sand.

Everything is happening now as it must.
All our oars are thrashing towards Dendera.
The ship is forging ahead on the water as if on a thousand feet.

The Limestone Girl

The limestone girl weathered by sun
no longer knows what life gave.
Proudly she was seated on the rock chair
raised above life, fate and grave.
Clad in her ancient clinging wrap
she stares past you towards death's wave.

Li Kan's Leave-taking beneath the Tree

I have come from Takalan to say goodbye.
There's a feel of autumn in the wind
a feel of autumn too in the wanderer.
Many years have gone since we last sat here.
The tree doesn't have the same leaves.
We don't have the same hair or skin.
What we first notice are the absent and the dead.
Our crowd is now just three.

Among those who have moved on through the passes
is Li Ti.
He painted beautiful scenes of rivers and streams on Rain Mountain.
He perished on the way through the Lao-hu-Nan Passes.
He drowned in snow.

I myself first heard about it three years afterwards.
My wife Tien Fang, who was then still alive,
came in and carefully told me of his death.

I felt I had fallen down in a chasm.
We decided not to eat that day.

A year later in the month of good weather
we visited the pass where Li Ti had been found.
There were now only cliffs and desolate wind.

We lay three holy branches we had brought with us.

I talk about this
because memories of departed friends
and the memory of a loved wife
are more than wisdom.
What do we want with wisdom
when we are only three.

When we are now gathered,
we three who have survived,
let wisdom rest.
May the mirrored memories resonate in the lute.
Let us slowly drink of the wine and play the melancholy song
of the lonely Water-Lantern on the River Lu.

Winter Night

We listened to the ice-waste out there.
Jammed by the cold it had begun to bellow.
Wanted out of the grip it had been pressed down into
but exhausted like someone confessing something
under the compulsion of thumbscrews.
Then it was silent again
and winter held its sway.

Islossning

Insjön får hjälp av blåst och sol,
börjar genast skrota ner sin vinter.
Losskurna isplåtar bogseras av vinden
utåt mot öppen mittström där de sänkas i tusental.
Solen är överallt med och trampar med glädje ner sig,
än här, än där.
Det suckar i sörjan, och fräser som i ett lutkar.

Ice Breaking Up

The lake gets help from gale and sun,
begins at once to demolish its winter.
Unscrewed sheets of ice are towed by the wind
out to the open midstream where they founder in their thousands.
The sun's in the middle of everything
and joyfully tramples itself down
now here, now there.
The slush sighs, seethes like a tub of lye.

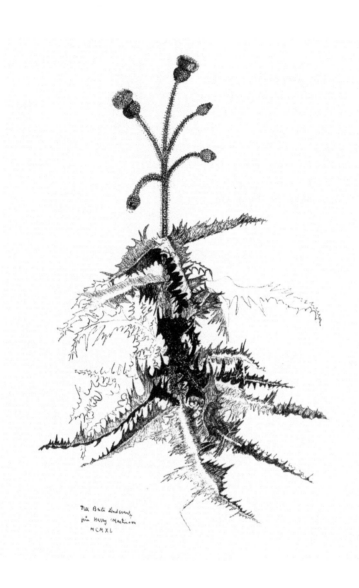

Till Birte Lindcrantz
från Harry Martinson
MCMXL

POEMS ON LIGHT AND DARKNESS
DIKTER OM LJUS OCH MÖRKER
(1971)

The World Clock

Heavily the seas eat at time's mountains
and the mountains are gathered in time's seas.
Where the forest was, valleys of the fish deepen.
Where the seas lay, the cool forest rustles.
The world clocks tick and space glitters.
Everything changes place and order.
Yet they are counted, the world's hours,
on Gaurisankar, in the ocean trough.

The Refugee

The refugee who fell back dead
and lay still for three days
on the remotest stretch of the plain
was visited towards evening on the third day
by the angel of frost.
She made ready his bier for the winter.
She beat loose with her mighty pinions
a fall of snow from the clouds.
It covered him, and the angel of frost winged away.
She made of his death
what frost can.
With spring, reality came back,
the first and greatest of the angels of death.

Victory in Babylon

From the ruler's feared mouth rose a cry, a command.
A captain relayed it. The army sent up an army bellow.
With great shrieks they battled for days and nights.
The war was won and the captives who had survived
were herded to the victor's city.

The sun shone when the troops reached home.
Terrified captives walked tense and exhausted.
Now the victims of the avenger were to die
so that the might of the ruler
could be mirrored in the blood of prisoners
on the streets of Babel.

The Winter Fly

The light comes back
sometimes sulphur yellow strips
can be seen and mile-long fire-pennants
stretched across the ice heaven
as if wanting to warm it.
We carefully watch a fly
which has wakened on the south window.
She lets a conversation unwind about her
humble fate and flies over to the stove.
There she listens for long to our thunderous voices.
The giants are clearly at home.

News

Bottle with a note
itself as passenger
bobbed in the North Atlantic
for seventeen years.
Silently and continuously referred
to a giant steamer from Southampton.
Ran aground unread and froze in
in the ice round Labrador.

Farmstead of the Pious

For more than a century
the gable window looked out on meadow and field.
The ground shone differently as time passed.
The years seemed to gather grass slowly
in thin clumps, meadow and field became tussocky,
ground moss sneaked in
from spruce shade.
The forest trees nudged closer
young pines appeared in the meadow.
At last it was clear to the gable's eye
that those who had worked the soil
had left the world at some point
from the other side of the house.
They had moved away
to a place on earth
to the farmland of heaven
with the singing of great bells.

The Last Load

The last harvest load creaked home.
The fields lay stubby and chill.
An old woman straggled after, distressed
by all that had no chance of staying.

The Jellyfish

The jellyfish moves, widens and breathes
in the heaving of the waves
in the surge from ebb and flow.
In it I saw the bowl from Tyrus
and every shape of the art of glass
Venice learned from the sea.
The glass bell-shape cupping itself translucently
becomes the bowl which is elongated
most elegantly into vase,
bulged out to tureen,
widened to be once more the dish in the sea,
the beautifully formed glass dish from Venice.

The Snowstorm

On the ridge in the spruce forest
lie ice-age boulders.
They have preserved the hard serenity
of gneiss and granite.

Each year the winter cold arrives
on snowstorm wings
packs snow round her wards
from deeper ages of winter.

She has not forgotten them.
Once she held them in a long embrace
in a time before the Yoldia Sea.

Hällristningen

Flydda språk som ljöd kring offrens tjurar
kan vi aldrig ana eller finna.
Ord för skördeväder, hagelskurar
har gått bort med ord för man och kvinna.
Hur lät namnet på den långa båten,
revbensspantad, avklätt tydligt ristad.
Hur lät ordet mjölk, vad hette solen.
Hur lät kärlekssången, sinnesorden,
ord för ögon, näsa, mun och öra,
sommarorden som i språket levde,
vinterordens snö och höstens äpple?
Hur lät namnet på den tunga döden.
Vi kan se, men vi kan inte höra.

The Rock Carving

Sounding round the offertory bulls, vanished language
we can never guess at or find.
Words for harvest weather, hail storms
have gone with words for man and woman.
How did the name sound for the long ship,
the rib-frame carved clearly.
How did the name sound for milk, what was the sun called.
How did the love-song sound, the words of the senses,
words for eyes, nose, mouth and ear,
the summer words alive in the language,
winter's snow-word and autumn's apple?
What did weighty death sound like.
We can see but we can't hear.

The Thrall Woman

The thrall woman still hummed tonelessly
where she stood by the grain stooped and weary
with her pestle, watching how the ears
slowly whitened to her pounding.
Tired and with aching fingers she grasped
her grinding stone so that she herself could live
a few more days of summer.
Butterflies flew up from the thrall quarters,
sparkled, became silent words inside her,
bright sun words she taught her children
when they came begging gruel by the mortar.

The Giant Lizard

In the Late Jurassic lived Brachiosaurus,
the four-legged giant wading lizard
the biggest and heaviest beast on earth.

Its gait was massive and ponderous,
its legs five times as long and thick
as those of an elephant – if elephants had existed –
for this gross-boned creature lived
half a million years before the elephant.

Its habitat was the coastal lagoons
and the enclosed lagoon lakes
along the shores of the Jurassic Sea
and the delta landscape whose flowing branches
would later petrify into stone branches
in the geological strata.

It lived off the floating water pest of its time
and off slimy algae abundantly filling
the shallow and wide-stretched lagoon flats
which were constantly topped up by the ever-
multiplying mass of algae as the giant ate.

Where this colossus had been at work
the stench of the closed-in stagnant lakes
lessened or vanished.
It worked as it ate, like a living lumbering
street-sweeping tank,
a Cleansing Department of its age, in the Jurassic lagoons.

Fossil bones of the giant, that oversized cleaner
so far before his time,
have been found in the strata of the Tendaguru Beds.

The Omen

The Tatars stopped their wagons and put up their tents.
From pure springs tracked down in inviting groves
water was fetched. A fresh stream tumbled forth, gave fishes.

Out of a tree a bird with beautiful plumage descended.
Its eyes and neck suggested it loved life.
Only with doubt and trembling it let itself be killed.

Roasted, it lay with its legs tied to its body.
Everyone looked at it, ready to enjoy it.
The strong gums smacked round each bite,
the teeth ground stolidly as life's own mills.

Too late, the Tatars discovered
their mistake:
they had roasted and eaten the Phoenix,
which in that season was vulnerable and mortal,
the finely plumed bird Fong from Tsin.

They had little time for regret
for a great darkness fell on the earth.
The sun began to be quenched.
Terrified, the shamans cried
that what had happened was an omen
and the Tatars lashed a few prisoners to death.
Then the sun emerged and all who had hidden
rushed out of their tents rejoicing.
But that same year Khan lost the war
against the general from Tsin.

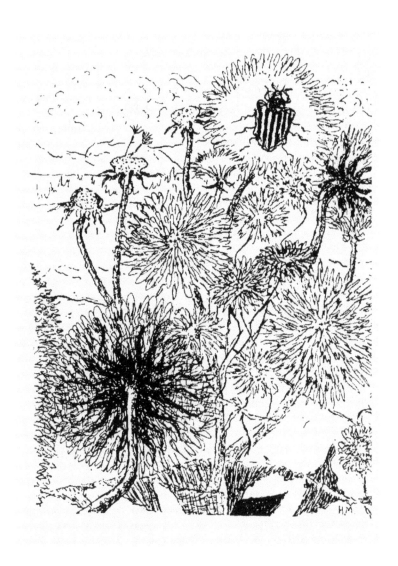

TUSSOCKS
TUVOR
(1973)

*

Spruce stands bole by bole with spruce.
They wrap themselves together
hold a needly brim over the twin-flower bells.
The flight of the grass-moth is low and fluttering
with unheard wingbeats.
Here the Nordic forest whispers
its least song.

*

A crooked spruce fringed with drooping lichen
grows old crammed against the gneiss.
The rock wall it stands beside
dressed to greyness so many
spruces which now mouldering
form an earth callus round the rock's stone foot
no one can count them.
No one can count the years of the stone wall
or how many forests it has met with blunt brow.
It just presses down on the wanderer's mind
with the weight of its melancholy wave.

*

The pine the tall mast-tree
with its crown like a mast-top
scanning our endless inner sea of spruce
where year from year and wave by wave
until our dying day we can count
how spruce is lost sight of among spruce.
All round us this our gloom-spreading enemy
and our rustling friend.
What would our world be without spruce trees,
without wood-pulp, Christmas tree and graveside sprig.
What would it be without the spruce-shelter
and without the shadowy tales
which can be told only by spruce.
We seek out the light of clearings
and live, in a way, in cities
where we imagine we are ourselves.
Still we are what we are
a spruce forest people
and with spruce we shall be buried.
Homelessly at home in cities and villages
we live with our melancholy immersed in spruce.
The spruces rustle.
Heavy with reality and with the sigh of spruce tales
they have command of our years
and shelter the needle-dark spirit
sighing within us,
our spirit of spruce.

*

The swamp mosses drink of the stream
until it is more and more low-voiced.
It sinks its watery clucking
to a summer whisper, drowned out by midges.
It soon changes to sign language,
which every tussock knows.
Soon its hidden meaning blossoms up
in moist buckbean.

*

Sideways sunlit
the ground in the clearing is a gold floor
and its grass a sun fleece.
In the midst of this forest chamber
the ancient boulder stands like a sturdy sideboard
with the key turned from inside
and moss in the lock.

*

Living the flycatcher life.
Seeing the bark-white nesting box
approach more and more often
with the bubble of hunger from inside,
insatiable and white
like a pinned up bill
to be paid fly by fly.
To swoop and snap
from early must-have morning
to stuffed-full time
when the nesting box bubble dies out.
So much the cost of life
in flycatcher groves.

*

After dew-fall
the snail began his journey
dressed in prune overcoat and with listening horn.
He took his busy way on the long road
towards the glade of ferns.
But paused every second ell
and rested quietly.
Now came the higher world
rollicking home from the dance.
The snail shrank
and lay black and diminished in the tussock.
The earth shook long and heavily
and the night wore late.
When the meadow soil stopped trembling
morning had arrived.

*

The struggle for life, and peace in the evening
coincide at sunset.
The whirr of the meadows and farflung weapon-rattling
fall silent in the grassy tussocks.
The blackbird holds a beautiful speech about ceasefires.
Cool as dew the coffin-black snail inspects
traces of the day that was.

Millwheels

Millwheels long since mouldered
turn freshly in dreams.
Memory still sees its millwheels
draped in watery veils.
Moist ferns sway round the mill-race.
Only when our memory has been stilled
do its mills stop turning.
Then only stones recall
older than raven or sybil
how from the hurrying water
millstones picked up speech.

The Quagmire

Here a blossoming quagmire carpet
was spread over pitch-black mud.
Remained viscous and wholly obliging
until it saw, too often, ill-will come
to spit in its water-lily.
It burst.
Opened an abyss
beneath ill-will's heel.

*

When the dew is raised by the sun
the meadow insects strike up,
each moment changing place
with high-pitched vibrato.
Their whirring lasts for hours.
Puffs of wind stir grass, play with light.
But the snails hang back all day
in unaltered shade.
Not until late evening do they set out,
heading then to a nearby grove,
a distant land.

*

In a house a clock struck midnight.
The sky was starry but from the north
mist was seen veering in and winding
its vapours round each branch.
Next morning rime clothed the forest.
Lightly on the grass dense and white hung
long rows of frozen water-drops
threaded so neatly on every stalk
as if in finger-play with the frost
they had chosen to bind glass-bead garlands.

*

Klar vintermorgon med snöiga grenverk.
Vinden har ännu en timme benådat
all skönhet höjd mot himmelen.
En gång, ja många såg jag samma syn
som nästan bara är en snötanke.
Minnets flingor församlade.
Tiderna föll som ömtålig grensnö.
Tidens flyktighet kunde räknas, som nu
flinga för flinga av vinden.

*

Clear winter morning with snowy branches.
The wind has for one more hour reprieved
all beauty raised heavenwards.
Once, often, I saw this,
almost a snow-thought.
The flakes of memory gathered.
The times fell like fragile snow from branches.
Time's fleetingness could be counted, as now
flake after flake by the wind.

*

Rime, winter's dew, clothes the forest branches.
Spruce in iron, birches in silver.
A few freezing bullfinches puff up
red in lilac bushes downy with frost.
Last year's grass glitters winter-salted.

*

Late-born swarms of flying creatures
set out beneath trees now leafless.
They pause in sheltered places
and are seen dancing up and down
where the autumn sun still gives warmth.
No one can tell their name or kind
before the autumn wind scuffs them out of the year,
out into homeless oceans of air.

If each one of them could be called a word,
then a life's language blows away on the wind.
Life and death, those two grand wasters,
play in the night with high stakes.
Uncounted and numberless most of what we see whirls
always away, a ceaseless scattering.

POSTHUMOUSLY PUBLISHED POEMS

Wilderness

On the distant plains
where spruce country thins out to moorland,
on the tufts grow dwarf cornel, the cornelian cherry of the moors.
It is so remotely silent here
in the day-bright summer nights
that the midges sound like radio voices.
In forest grass and heath sedges
the memory of a path hides,
a path which once led here
on plank walkways long since
mouldered and rotted to wood powder.
Here even the hunger of absence is gone.
Not one single longing reaches this far.
Forest and moor lead everything astray,
almost on purpose.
Wilderness speaks to wilderness
in summer tongue or winter speech.
The forest takes all winds as they come.
Picks out at last what still becomes
the north winds, the snowfalls,
the snow that lies till June.

*

In the attic windows with their diagonal cracks
glimmer age-yellowed newspapers from the Sarajevo year.
The dust on the attic floor rolls, gathers.
Acquires spindly hair legs and scuttles about.
With each draught from the wrenched open door they stir
scramble off with the shadows.
The agile dust-spiders flit each time the old woman
comes up for some of the more-than-over-ripe apples for dessert.
She posed as a young bride the same year
as a bullet, according to the now yellowed paper,
felled Ferdinand of Hapsburg.

*

The churchyard grass rustles widely in Europe.
The cicada strikes up on some classical cemetery,
its cousin the cricket answers high on some northern heath.
For a few brief summers the ear listens to
the brief cricket lives and ground-level songs
and one day the last cricket is there.
Then the meadows fall silent,
that fine ancient death
takes the mole's path down
to the underworld.

Preying Dragonflies

Built for the life-breath of battle
they eat in battle,
their meal is an assault.
Ingeniously contrived as
weapons of ambush
themselves living projectiles
they pick their target with an exact instinct
swoop on it
and eat it in mid-air.
If the catch is filling enough
they land fleetingly
on a leaf above water
and present for a minute
a still picture
on the water mirror.

*

Richly endowed with genus-knack
and knowing all their p's and q's
nature's very tiniest work away
well practised in shadowy and sunny places.
In each tussock a swarm of specialists,
on each and any stalk
a fly with finely tuned instinct.
Signals are sent out non-stop
from punctilious measuring creeping things.
All the signals are snatched up instantly.
Each moment is precious for everyone.
They all want to keep
their grip on surviving the hour,
just possibly the day

*

The clouds of rainy days withdraw
and the sun is exposed.
The rainbow builds itself
for a few frail minutes
with shimmering foundations sunk
in spruce forest and lakes.
Although sky high and huge
it weighs less than a midge.

*

The gaze searches in the forest grass,
picks out an ant as a wandering now-point
climbs with it down among stalks.
The wind fidgets in the grass
the gaze looses its chosen now-point.
The moments have glided
apart, are confused.
The minute is gone in the tussock.
But the moss round about smells of years
and the low-topped stones of centuries.

In Summer

In summer there's no cow out on the ice
and blue thundercloud berries can be plucked in the woods.
The wild strawberry bleeds on the tongue with no blood.
Then life is fully occupied
being what it is: an attempt at paradise.

Along the Echo's Paths

Back along the echo's paths.
There the words rest in the box of their old meanings.
But how alien. What are they saying, those lips.
They speak of other contexts and conditions.
While you listen to their talk
they shape something which is changed also by them
they spell in a language even further away
in yet another of the little boxes
in the mountain of the seven boxes
thousands and thousands of years before Babylon.

*

In childish years
the islet is a many-masted ship.
All the leaf sails are set.
The day itself sets out on the mirror and catches the wind.
The sun lays on a light-party in the water-summer.
The senses are off on an imaginary fishing trip in the wind.

*

Once upon a time I went to paradise. It was empty. An abandoned village in a remote leafy wood.

Even the school house was up for letting. But no one came.

The local road narrowed as the grass wandered in from the verges. Yet there still hovered here a sense of humanity. Something like that persists. The schoolchildren were out for a break, playing noisily. It was just that they could not be seen. Like their teacher they were invisible. And now she walked towards me. I could see that because the grass gave way to her invisible steps. She stopped in front of me and I looked into her eyes. They were the skies above the forest. When she greeted me with a few words I heard that her voice was the wind blended with birdsong. One step more and I myself would have been, like her, invisible. When at last I walked away I heard her calling. Three times she called in paradise.

Reconciliation

In a village were I lived there was a farmer I hated. I decided that before I left the place I would throw a stone in his face. One evening I spotted him driving home from work with his horse and cart. I stood in among some trees, out of his sight. But suddenly he drew in the horse and stopped the ramshackle cart.

He sat quite still for a long time and gradually I realised that he was listening to the very silence of the evening around him, to that tranquillity which can be heard only by someone who is alone. I sidled away.

*

Sharpened by the moon's cold sheen
the snow glare dazzles the windows,
crawls sheet-white in across silent floors.
When the clock strikes it sounds
as if it were beyond the bounds of life.

*

Felled –
the avenue of golden willows
that shone in cold blue springs.
Leaning over the windy road
they glowed mimosa-soft above the ditch
where the earth was still iron-blue,
the surface of the fields like slag-heaps,
the cry of cranes like
the whine of the circular saw.

*

Sticky yellow in the eye
the marsh marigold lights
spring's first cool lamp.
Led by its sheen
the wind searches long
for summer's door
which hides in the shadow beneath the alder.

*

The sky didn't squander hail-blasts this year.
Instead, over the army of the wheat is heard
the combine harvester's thunder.
Decisively and mechanically it gulps forward,
an alien body highly profitable,
a heavy prose-box of reality
spouting chaff like numbers.

*

There's a species of dry truths,
the important small ones that don't bleed,
that don't moisten the eye or paint themselves
there as beautiful pictures.
Nor do they bribe
the ear with resonances.
Those truths are like straw and stones,
like simple yes and no
and brick-rough bread.

*

The smart-and-sly fox
I often watch
on early mornings in summer
while the houses still night-blind
yet windowed big-eyed
sleep by the morning lake.

Smart-and-sly sidles out of the wood swerved by his tail.
He listens his way from tussock to tussock
playfully ear-pricked,
smiling as in a fable
he bow-springs on the spot,
sets his front paws together
on the right clutch-point
and nips the bewildered morning vole.

Ärlan

Ärlan i ständig vippning
letar och spanar
stannar till och vickar ner,
intar genskjutarställning
och låter insekten själv flyga emot,
snappar till.
Upprepar knepet, vippar, vänder sig,
tricksar sidleds.
Samlar näbbgreppsvis portionerna,
packar och jämkar.
Med den tryggt fastknipna födan
som en mustasch kring näbben
flyger hon till boet.

The Wagtail

The wagtail perpetually wagging
searches and spies
stops dead and tips down,
acts the interceptor
and lets the insect come straight on,
snaps up.
Repeats the trick, bobs, twists,
dodges sideways.
Collects beak-snap-wise the portions,
packs and jabs.
With the firmly grasped feed
like a moustache round its beak
flicks off to the nest.

*

The reed stalk stands wronged against but erect
and on the water mirror
its shadow flicks like a whiplash.

*

The motion of the shadowing clouds
is felt right down in the earth.
When late-summer days cloud over
the ground cools to the chill of a cellar.
The grass around us darkens before it yellows.
The wellspring sharpens its iron taste.

*

The wind searched in the forest grass
and found a word,
it sounded like unsayable life
but it was a name the biggest stone gave
to the smallest twilight butterfly.
Too hard to remember says the wave.
Too fine to be said flickers the wind.

TRANSLATOR'S NOTE

These translations are the result of a project initiated and guided by a group of Sweden's foremost experts in Harry Martinson's work, and I would like to record my gratitude to them for help both in interpreting some of the texts and in facilitating the practical aspects of completing the project. The group consisted of:

Göran Bäckstrand, who has long professional experience in diplomacy and international relations, has for many years held various offices in the Harry Martinson Society. His connection with the Society is now less formal but no less active.

Kjell Espmark, Professor Emeritus of Stockholm University and member of the Swedish Academy, has published not only scholarly works but also fiction and poetry.

Johan Lundberg, Associate Professor in Literature at Stockholm University, is Editor-in-Chief of *Axess* magazine.

Staffan Söderblom, Professor of Creative Writing at Gothenburg University, is well-known as author, translator and critic.

Harry Martinson is the subject of two critical studies by Espmark, one by Söderblom and a doctoral thesis by Lundberg.

R.F.